Family Walks in the Lincolnshire Wolds and Marshes

Camilla Harrison

HIGH INTEREST LOW MILEAGE

Scarthin Books of Cromford
Derbyshire
1997

For Stella, with love and with memories of Mum.

THE COUNTRY CODE

Guard against all risk of fire
Fasten all gates
Keep dogs under proper control
Keep to paths across farmland
Avoid damaging fences, hedges and walls
Leave no litter
Safeguard water supplies
Protect wildlife, plants and trees
Go carefully on country roads
Respect the life of the countryside

Published by Scarthin Books, Cromford, Derbyshire, 1997

Phototypesetting by Techniset Typesetters, Newton-le-Willows, Merseyside WA12 9YE

Printed by Redwood Books

Maps by Ivan Sendall

Cover photograph: Tealby (Route 3). Courtesy Lincolnshire County Council

Other photographs by the author

ISBN 0-907758-67-3

Preface

Arise and let us wander forth,
To yon old mill across the wolds;
For look the sunset, south and north,
Winds all the vale in rosy folds.

Alfred Tennyson.

The landscape of the wolds and the marsh provided the inspiration for Tennyson's best rustic poetry. He remembered the 'calm and deep peace on this high wold', in a childhood that was often unhappy. In *Ode to Memory* he describes the serenity of the southern wolds and the Lymn Valley, and the isolated beauty of the North Sea coast.

The wolds have seen some changes since Tennyson lived in the Rectory at Somersby. The winding lanes are surfaced now, the car has arrived, the farm machinery is no longer dependent on horse power. But there have been no major building developments, no large industrial projects, no motorway networks. The 'deep peace' is largely undisturbed and the natural beauty of the wolds intact.

Even the marsh, 'stretched wide and wild', is on the whole unspoilt, with only a narrow band of tourist development from Skegness to Mablethorpe.

... A sand built ridge
Of heaped hills that mound the sea,
Overblown with murmers harsh
... A lowly cottage whence we see
Stretched wide and wild the waste enormous marsh,
Where from the frequent bridges,
Like emblems of infinity,
The trenched waters run from sky to sky.

Alfred Tennyson

About the author
Camilla Harrison has had long associations with the Lincolnshire countryside and has been drawn particularly to the beauty of the wolds and the isolation of the marsh. She has been writing about rural issues for a number of years and is the author of Family Walks in the Teme Valley (Scarthin Books). She is a part-time English teacher and has five children.

Acknowledgements
I would like to thank Stella and Peter Millburn and their children, Edwin, Robbie and Rose for their help and hospitality during the writing of this book. Particular thanks to Stella for companionship and to Peter for advice on local history.

Thanks also to Jane and Nick Wise for their hospitality and to Edwin and Wendy Roper for their advice on local recipes.

I would also like to thank Lindsay Summers and Susan Scarth for their help with childcare, and to thank Susan Scarth for the use of the typewriter.

Many thanks to my husband, Bob and to my children, Aidan, Sylvia, Bronwyn and Tom for their support, companionship and understanding.

Map of Area

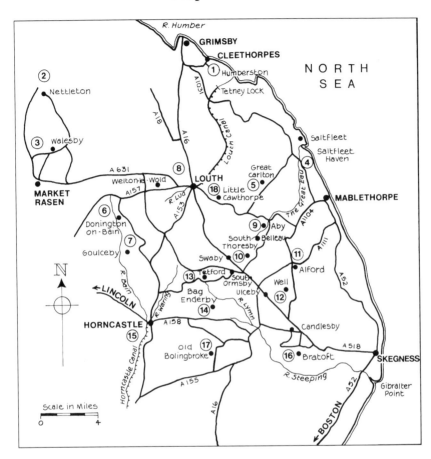

Contents

Dunes and salt marsh (Route 4).

Introduction

From the North West the Lincolnshire Wolds rise steeply from the Moor, the ironstone crags rust brown on the skyline. These are the highest wolds, the steep valley sides scarred with ancient mine workings. From the South the approach is softer. The Wolds rise gently from the Fens, the land is more easily farmed and the river valleys of the Bain, the Waring and the Lymn lead between rolling hillsides of chalk grassland. From the East across the Marsh the wolds mark an ancient shoreline, extended over millions of years, first by the glaciers and then by the efforts of men and women to reclaim land from the sea. The medieval shoreline is marked by the A1031 that leads through Marsh Chapel and Saltfleet.

The Lincolnshire Wolds are now a Designated Area of Outstanding Natural Beauty. The rolling hills form part of the chalk belt that stretches from Dorset to Yorkshire and are only 550 feet above sea level at their highest point. The landscape is dominated by the skyline – scarecrows on horizons of bare earth can create a bleakness here in the winter months – but under a blue sky alive with lark song the scene changes, the skyline becomes vibrant with the growing crop and the views across the marsh or to distant ridges of the wolds shimmer in the salt tinged air.

The Lymn is the prettiest of the Wolds rivers, fast flowing over a gravelly bed, unpolluted by industry and leading through spinneys and beneath old stone bridges. This was the river of Tennyson's childhood, the source of some of his finest poetry.

The landscape is criss-crossed by disused railway lines and canals from the long gone days of industry and by the becks and streams leading along the valleys to the main rivers, as they lead off the Wolds and out across the Marsh and the Fen to the North Sea. The Great Eau rises at the edge of the Wolds in Belleau and flows across the Marsh to Saltfleet Haven. It was diverted there in the Middle Ages in an attempt to prevent the haven from silting up.

The coastline becomes quite heavily developed from Theddlethorpe to Skegness. Although this stretch can hardly be described as beautiful, there is an enormous amount of things to do with children on rainy days – indoor swimming pools, cinemas, roller skating rinks and various wildlife centres.

The Wolds and the Marsh have a strong sense of the past, of time in many dimensions. A Roman road, the High Street, leads from Horncastle to Lincoln and another route from Lincoln to Skegness, much of which is accessible as a bridleway or footpath. The Bluestone Heath Road was in use as a trackway long before the Roman invasion – a prehistoric route following a bleak and treeless ridge of the wolds. Once the track led above impenetrable forest. Now the valleys are farmed and settled, the village names standing as testament to the Viking invaders who decided to stay in Lincolnshire and cultivate the land, Calceby and Calcethorpe, Ketsby and Driby. Later in the fourteenth century many of these thriving settlements suffered the effects of the Black Death – all that now remains of Calceby are the ruins of the chalk-built church and the earth mounds of the deserted homesteads.

To the East of the Bluestone Heath Road Louth spire can be glimpsed between the hills. You can go up inside the spire with the consent of the vicar and look out over the

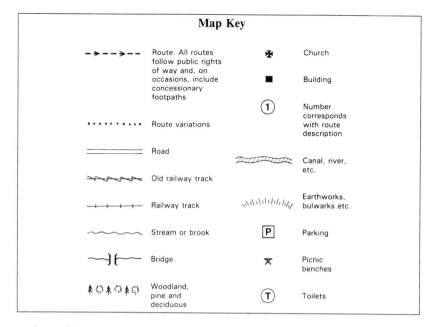

Map Key

➤ ➤ ➤ Route. All routes follow public rights of way and, on occasions, include concessionary footpaths	✠ Church
	■ Building
• • • • • • • • • Route variations	① Number corresponds with route description
══════ Road	〰〰〰〰 Canal, river, etc.
⋞⋞⋞⋞ Old railway track	
┼ ┼ ┼ ┼ Railway track	╲╲╲╲╲╱╱ Earthworks, bulwarks etc.
〜〜〜〜 Stream or brook	P Parking
─┤├── Bridge	⋊ Picnic benches
♠♧♠♧♠♧ Woodland, pine and deciduous	Ⓣ Toilets

rooftops of the town to the surrounding countryside. The town has some particularly lovely architecture and its centre is a conservation area.

Further south lies the town of Alford with its five-sail working windmill, thatched manor house and tales of smugglers. Horncastle, in the crook of the Bain and the Waring is a good town for browsing. It has an enormous number of antique and bric-a-brac shops and there are definitely bargains to be found.

This part of Lincolnshire has been fairly isolated from the rest of the country, the regional dialect is better preserved here than anywhere else in England and much of the land is still owned by the families that came over with the Norman Conquest.

The Walks

I've tried to include all the varieties of the landscapes of the wolds and marsh in these routes. Where possible, the uphill stretches are at the start of the walk, to make life easier for families with young children. Pocket nature guides can add an interesting dimension, too, and can be used to check up on potential edibles found growing along the route. All the walks in this book can be found on the Ordnance Survey Landranger maps 113 Grimsby and 122 Skegness.

Tetney Haven

Outline

Tetney Haven RSPB Reserve – sea wall – Tetney lock – Waithe Beck – Tetney Haven.

Summary

This is a walk of historical and natural interest commanding wide views of saltmarsh reaching to the North Sea, where the oil tankers loom large on the horizon.

Attractions

The RSPB Reserve at Tetney Haven is open all year round and welcomes visitors. Walks on the reserve itself are sometimes accompanied by the warden, who lives on the site in a small portacabin. The reserve covers 3,000 acres of saltmarsh, sand dunes and mud flats, and provides habitat for many rare shore birds. Of particular interest is a colony of little terns which can often be seen hovering above the many creeks in search of fish or crustaceans. Shelduck and redshank, oystercatchers and ringed plovers are to be seen here amongst the dunes and on the open marsh along with the predatory hen harriers and merlins.

In the last century Tetney Haven sheltered ships that were waiting to sail up the Louth canal. The ships brought in timber and coal and carried out wool and corn. The arrival of the East Coast railway in 1848 led to the canal redundancy and by the 20th century it was completely disused. The canal is now a useful land drain and a collector for Covenham Reservoir.

There is another interesting Nature Reserve at the nearby village of Tetney. Here, there are some extraordinarily deep blow holes, amidst spinneys of poplar, from which beautiful crystal clear water flows. Tales abound locally about carriages with six horses and fine gentry being swallowed up in the hole, never to be seen again . . .

Route 1

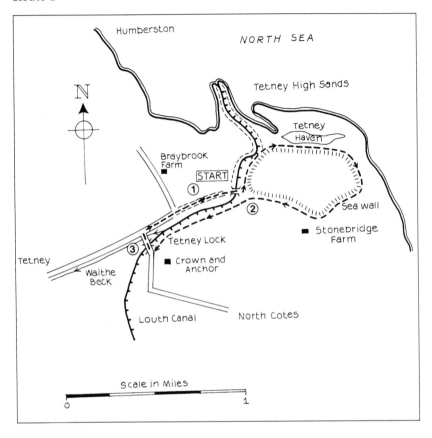

Humberston

NORTH SEA

N

Tetney High Sands

Tetney
Haven

Braybrook
Farm

START

①

②

Sea wall

Stonebridge
Farm

Tetney

Tetney Lock

③

Waithe
Beck

Crown and
Anchor

Louth Canal

North Cotes

Scale in Miles

0   1

Tetney Haven   2 miles

Start

At the RSPB Reserve, Tetney Haven. Heading north on the A1031 from Marsh Chapel, turn right for North Cotes and then left for Tetney Lock. Cross the bridge over the Louth Canal and turn right for Tetney Haven RSPB Reserve. Park in the Reserve. GR 343022, Landranger 113.

Route

1. *Cross the bridge over the canal and turn left. Follow the sea wall along the edge of Tetney Haven and above Stonebridge Farm.*

2. *On returning to the bridge, remain on the east side and follow the footpath along the Louth Canal. At the Crown and Anchor turn right over the road bridge. Cross the canal and Waith Beck.*

3. *Continue to the T-junction and turn right. Follow the track straight ahead and return to START.*

Refreshments

The Crown and Anchor provides a good selection of snacks and bar meals. There is a well-equipped childrens play area.

The Tetney Blowholes.

Nettleton Beck

Outline

Radio mast – Viking Way – Nettleton Beck – Quarry Tunnel – Lakes – Nettleton Grange – Salutation Inn – Nettleton Top – Radio Mast.

Summary

This is the highest part of the wolds, the steep sided valleys belying the popular myth that Lincolnshire is flat. The route follows the Viking Way along the banks of Nettleton Beck and includes a series of small lakes, a lovely stretch of deciduous woodland and some open meadows. Fossils can be found amongst the chalk.

Attractions

The wolds here have long been a source of iron ore. The Romans mined it during their occupation and the tradition continued up until the 1950s when the iron foundries at Scunthorpe began to import foreign ore. Local chalk is still quarried though, and used at the foundry in the smelting process. The old scars of the workings can still be seen on the valley sides. The adventurous may be tempted to explore the old quarry. If you scramble up the wooded bank over the tunnel and follow the disused steps upwards you arrive at a bricked-up tunnel in the hillside – local legend has it that an old traction engine and its driver were buried there when the walls collapsed years ago.

The Beck itself and the chalk grassland of the valley bottom provide habitats for wheatears and a variety of warblers and buntings. Yellow brimstone butterflies lay their eggs in the buckthorn bushes at the edge of the woodland and find sustenance amongst the clumps of nettles, along with peacocks, red admirals and the common blue.

A young Lincolnshire beauty, Rose Millburn of Driby, recommends the following Nettle Hair Tonic: Steep a good sized bunch of young spring nettles in a pan of boiling water. Leave to cool, and use as a final rinse on the hair for extra shine and lustre.

Peacocks wander freely around the garden of Nettleton Grange. Don't be alarmed by their rather bloodcurdling shrieks!

The walk back along the lane has the benefit of some fine views across the moor towards Lincoln. The verges are wide and safe for walking and are a mass of cowslips, tufted vetch and bugle in the early summer. Nevertheless it may be an idea for a willing adult to fetch the car, while children rest and paddle in the beck opposite Nettleton Grange.

Route 2

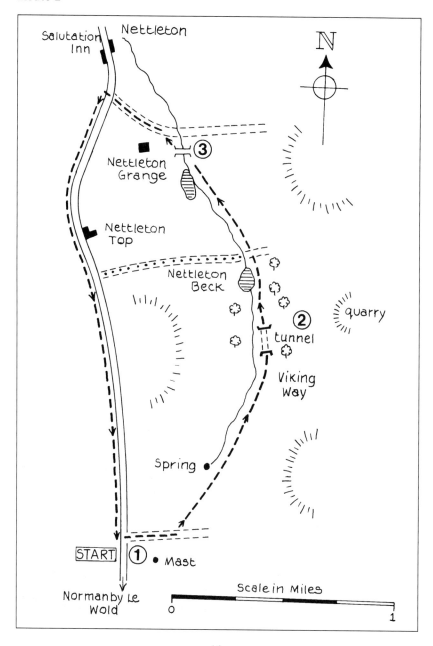

Route 2

Nettleton Beck

3¹/₂ miles

Start

On the A46, three miles South of Nettleton towards Normanby-le-Wold. Park on the verge beside the radio mast. Gr 115968. Landranger 113.

Route

1. *Facing the mast from the road follow the track to the left of it. Go through the gate then turn left along the Viking Way which is waymarked. Bear right towards the corner of the field. Cross the stile and walk along the right hand side of the hedge and the stream bed.*

2. *Follow the path through the tunnel and on through the woodland. Pass a lake to your left. At the edge of the wood, turn left onto the track, then right over the stile into the meadow. Follow the path alongside the stream and past the lakes.*

3. *Cross the bridge. Continue to the junction with the track, then turn left. Follow the track past Nettleton Grange and out onto the lane. Turn right for the Salutation Inn at Nettleton or turn left and walk back to the car, along the wide grass verge.*

Nettleton

Refreshments

Children are welcome at the Salutation Inn. There is a beer garden with children's play area and a menagerie. Bar snacks are available, along with good quality three course meals. The pub is listed in the CAMRA good food guide and the Brett Collier guide.

Nettle Beer

100 nettle stalks
2^1/$_2$ gallons of water
3 lb sugar
2 oz of Cream of Tartar
^{1}/$_2$ oz of yeast

Boil the nettles in the water for 15 minutes. Strain and add the Cream of Tartar and the sugar. Heat and stir the liquid until the sugar has dissolved. Remove from the heat and leave until tepid. Then add the yeast, cover with a cloth and leave for 24 hours. Scrape off the scum, bottle and cork.

Ringlet butterfly on a nettle

16

Walesby to Tealby

Outline
Walesby – Catskin Lane – Risby Manor Farm – Castle Farm – Tealby – River Rase – Tealby Tearooms – Castle Farm – Risby Manor Farm – The Ramblers' Church – Walesby.

Summary
The route leads through good hill country and deciduous woodland to the picturesque village of Tealby on the River Rase. The ford across the river is a popular paddling spot for local children.

Attractions
Tealby derives from the Anglo-Saxon word for a chessboard or table, 'taefl' which in this instance would have referred to the flat topped hill across the side of which the village is scattered. The 'by' is of course Scandinavian – probably the Vikings took over an established Anglo-Saxon settlement. After the Norman invasion the Scandinavian land owners were replaced by Normans, one of whom was William the Conqueror's half brother, Bishop Odo of Bayeux. The name of the ruined Bayon's Manor derives from this name. The manor should have been inherited by Alfred Tennyson's father, but he was dispossessed in favour of his younger brother. It was in Tealby in 1807 that a lucky ploughman discovered over 5,000 silver pennies of Henry II's reign buried in an earthenware pot near the Caistor High Street. Perhaps they were buried there by a traveller who never returned to unearth them. A sample of the coins can be seen in the British Museum, but their mystery remains unsolved.

There is an open access area in the fields surrounding Risby Manor Farm. The public are free to wander in this area, which makes a good picnic spot, but care must be taken to avoid damaging fences or frightening livestock. On a clear day there are fine views to the west across the moor, with Lincoln Cathedral an impressive feature on the skyline.

In the churchyard of the Rambler's Church there is a beacon to commemorate the arrival of the Spanish Armada and its subsequent defeat. The church holds a service every Trinity Sunday for hikers and cyclists, and there is a window in the church depicting Christ blessing an assorted group of ramblers.

Route 3

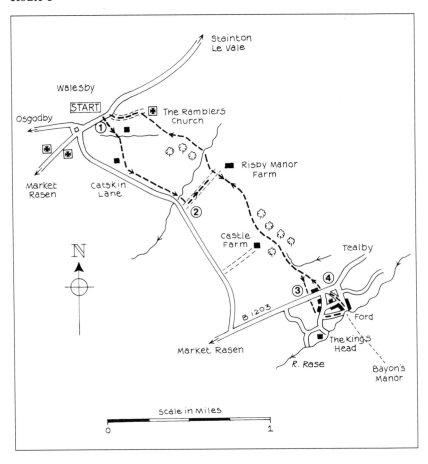

Route 3

Walesby to Tealby   4 miles

Start

At Walesby, which lies three miles north east of Market Rasen, just off the B1203. Park just below the driveway leading up to the Ramblers' Church, Walesby. This is at the bottom of Walesby Hill, at the eastern end of the village. GR 135923. Landranger 113.

Route

1. *Look for a gap in the wall below the driveway and follow the Public Footpath sign that directs you through this. Go along the edge of the garden and over the stile. Cross the stream and follow the path over the hill. Walk past the house, and head for the gate in the far hedge. Turn left onto Catskin Lane. Follow the lane for about half a mile until a bridleway leading left is reached.*

2. *Follow the bridleway up the hill towards Risby Manor Farm. Before reaching the farm, turn right onto the Viking Way footpath. Follow the path through the wood and past Castle Farm. Continue alongside the hedge then along the stream. Leave the stream and head on towards Tealby, keeping the hedge to your right. Follow the footpath between the houses and onto the road.*

3. *Cross the road and follow the footpath straight ahead, along the bottom of the gardens and out onto the lane. Turn right for the King's Head, then retrace your steps. To reach the ford over the River Rase go across the lane and down the Smooting. (From the ford a footpath leads right, to the remains of Bayon's Manor.) Turn left at the ford, then left again for the Tealby Tearooms. From the tearooms, continue to the end of the road and turn right. Cross the main road and join the Viking Way.*

4. *Follow the Viking Way back past Castle Farm. Go straight on past Risby Manor Farm and onto Walesby All Saints Church, otherwise known as the Ramblers Church. From the church follow the drive down to the road and turn left to finish.*

Refreshments

The King's Head at Tealby is a particularly pretty thatched pub with a large and well-tended beer garden. The usual sandwiches, snacks and bar meals are available throughout the year. The Tealby Tearooms adjoin the general store in the village and provide sandwiches, cakes and hot snacks. The tearooms are closed on Mondays, with the exception of Bank Holidays.

The Viking Way between Walesby and Tealby.

Saltfleet Dunes

Outline

Sea View Farm – Saltfleet Dunes – Black Gowt Sluice – Saltfleet Haven – The New Inn – Saltfleet – The Great Eau – Saltfleet Dunes – Sea View Farm.

Summary

The Saltfleetby – Theddlethorpe Dunes National Nature Reserve stretches along five miles of the Lincolnshire coast, and includes the highest and oldest dunes in the county. Paths wind between thickets of sea buckthorn, briar rose and blackthorn, or to the foreshore where dunlins and redshanks can sometimes be seen feeding on the mudflats. The village of Saltfleet has an interesting manor house, a disused windmill and a friendly pub, the New Inn.

Attractions

Between the dunes and the sea there is a mature salt marsh that was productive in medieval times. The salt was transported along the old Salters Way that leads from Grainthorpe to Lincoln. Now the marsh provides habitats for short-eared owls, red plovers and shelduck, wheeling swallows and skylarks. The bright orange berries of the female buckthorn provide sustenance for thrushes and field fares long into the winter months. The rare natterjack toad has burrows in the sand dunes. Listen for the chanting of the males in the spring and early summer, particularly on warm evenings. Beyond the salt marsh are the samphire beds – the samphire can be eaten either fresh or pickled.

The reserve is known locally as 'Rimac', after the wreck of a ship of this name. Wrecks were common along this coastline and played an important part in the culture of the area. On the dark side there are tales of the wreckers who deliberately misled ships into dangerous waters and then reaped the benefit of the cargo that was swept to shore. Bodies of sailors were stripped, their clothes and jewellery taken. On the other hand there are tales of extreme bravery, of human chains stretching out into stormy seas to rescue drowning men and of boats being launched in gale force winds in attempts to reach ships in peril.

Saltfleet itself was a popular bathing resort in the eighteenth century and still attracts summer visitors to a small caravan and chalet park. Before reaching the sands at Saltfleet the route leads down Haven Bank. This once busy North Sea port is badly silted up now, despite efforts in the Middle Ages to counteract this. The Great Eau was diverted in the fourteenth century from joining the North Sea below Rimac House, to swell the other streams that entered the Haven. The original course of the river can be seen on an Ordnance Survey map, but is hard to trace amongst the dunes.

The village has several interesting features. There is an impressive manor house in which Oliver Cromwell is said to have stayed after the Battle of Winceby and a beautifully tended Methodist chapel, surrounded by a well tended garden with seats for the weary.

Route 4

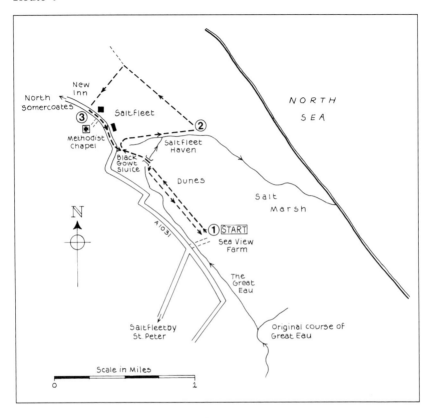

Route 4

Saltfleet Dunes   3¹/₂ miles

Start

Off the A1031 south from Saltfleet. The track for Sea View Farm is opposite the turning for Saltfleetby St. Peter. Park in the car park at Sea View Farm. GR 464924. Landranger Series 113.

Route

1. *Facing the sea turn left over the stile and follow one of the winding paths that lead through the dunes. Once off the dunes take the path leading straight ahead to Black Gowt Sluice. Cross the bridge, continue to the road, then turn right down Haven Bank.*

2. *Look out for the car park on your left. Turn left across the sand here, with the dunes to your left. Turn left after about half a mile and follow the track through the caravan site and alongside the New Inn.*

3. *Turn left onto the road. Walk through the village and turn left onto the footpath just beyond Haven Bank. Follow the path back over Black Gowt Sluice. Keep to the shore side of the dunes and return to Sea View Farm.*

Saltfleet Haven.

23

Refreshments
The New Inn is even bigger than the manor house but despite its size provides no sustenance other than crisps and peanuts, and a warm welcome. There is a shop in the village where sandwiches and drinks can be bought. The dunes provide beautifully sheltered picnic spots.

Pickled Marsh Samphire
Pick the young shoots of the plant during July and August, before they grow above 8 inches high. Chop these into 1 inch pieces, put them in a jar and cover with wine vinegar. Add a spoonful of fresh chopped herbs. Leave for two months before eating.

Saltfleet Haven.

24

Two Mile Bank

Outline
Sturdy Hill – Great Carlton – Eastfield Farm – Two Mile Bank – Sturdy Hill.

Summary
You can follow the Two Mile Bank all the way to Theddlethorpe All Saints – on a fine day, walking coastwards along the path, you may be tempted. The colours of the marsh are muted, understated in the perpetual misty haze that rises from the many drains and ditches and from the Great Eau that cuts across its centre. The path is at sea level, so there are no glimpses of the sea itself, lying behind the ancient bank of dunes that line the coast here.

Attractions
This land was reclaimed by the Romans in a massive draining programme. The rich soil produces a good variety of wild mushrooms in the autumn. We found shaggy ink caps along the bridleway. These are edible and delicious but don't drink alcohol with them – the combination causes severe stomach pains and vomiting.

The hedgerows of Two Mile Bank are old and long established – in late spring the blackthorn blossom and then the may are in bloom followed by a mass of briar roses in the summer. In autumn there are the fruits sloes, blackberries and rosehips. These can all be picked and made good use of in recipes or in winter floral displays.

The Two Mile Bank was a regular smugglers' route in the last century. Folklore has it that a particularly notorious band of 'owlers' was led by a local parson. He told the small-holders and cottagers who lived along the bank to bolt their doors and shutter their windows to cover their ears against strange nocturnal sounds, as these were the noises of the devil. The local people obeyed, but not the excise men who successfully caught the gang red-handed.

Water Rail

25

Route 5

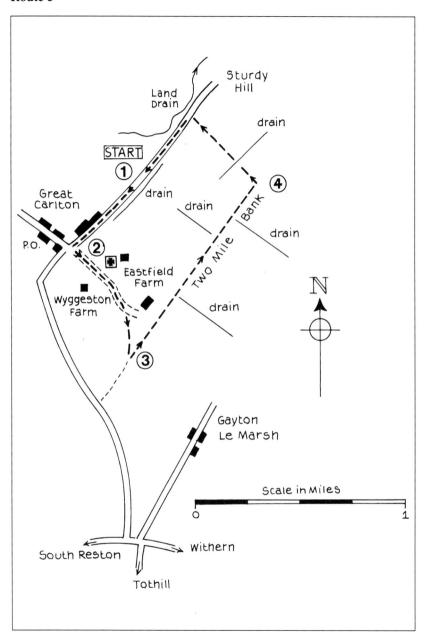

Route 5

Two Mile Bank   3 miles

Start

Great Carlton lies two miles north of the A157 between Louth and Alford. From the crossroads at Great Carlton head north-east along Sturdy Hill. After about half a mile park on the verge. GR 415855. Landranger 122.

Route

1. *Walk back along the lane to the road junction at Great Carlton.*

2. *Turn left here along a bridleway and pass Wyggeston Farm and Eastfield Farm. Just beyond Eastfield Farm go through the wooden gate and turn left onto Two Mile Bank bridleway.*

3. *Continue, with Eastfield Farm on the left, for one mile before taking a left turn up a marked public footpath.*

4. *Follow the path over a drain and continue to a road, Sturdy Hill. Turn left and walk along the road for half a mile back to the start.*

Refreshments

There are no refreshment stops on the route, other than the berried hedgerows in the autumn!

Sloe Jelly

2 lb of ripe sloes
2 lb of sugar
$^1/_2$ pint of water

Boil the sloes in the water until soft. Strain the liquid through a piece of old linen (a pillow case is ideal). Add the sugar to the juice and boil until setting point is reached, stirring all the time. Pour the jelly into clean jam jars and leave it to cool before putting the lids on. The jelly is delicious on bread, or as an accompaniment to roast fowl.

Shaggy inkcaps

27

The River Bain at Biscathorpe.

Donington to Biscathorpe

Outline

The Black Horse pub – Donington Water Mill – River Bain – Fishing Lakes – St. Helen's Church – Biscathorpe – River Bain – The Black Horse.

Summary

The route takes in a particularly pretty stretch of the River Bain and includes two private fishing lakes, havens for a variety of wild fowl. The Medieval village of Biscathorpe is typical of the many lost Lincolnshire settlements, and is a poignant testament to these once thriving communities.

Attractions

The River Bain rises to the north-west of Donington, near the site of the Medieval village of West Wykeham. It carves its way past Biscathorpe and on to Donington Mill, the site of a grisly murder in the last century. The murder victim, predictably a woman in white, is said to glide along the banks here after nightfall.

The Bain would obviously have been a vital source of sustenance to the Medieval wold dwellers of Wykeham and Biscathorpe. Up until the middle of the fourteenth century the arable land of these villages would have been cultivated in strips by the peasant farmers. The soil is not particularly fertile here but a vast proportion of the population of Lincolnshire at this time forced the cultivation of the wolds. No doubt then, the work would have been hard, the product meagre.

Late in the summer of 1348 the Black Death struck for the first time. Over the next thirty years more than a third of the population of England was wiped out. In some cases whole villages died. In others the few remaining survivors headed for the more fertile land of the marsh. There were no longer sufficient peasants to farm the marginal land of the wolds, and in time the land-owners demolished the mud-built villages and replaced the open field system with hedged enclosures for sheep and cattle. Lincolnshire has roughly two hundred of these lost villages, identifiable only by the grassy mounds that cover the ruins of peasant farmsteads and the depressions in between that mark the village paths.

The site of Biscathorpe is now a massive rabbit warren and a local picnic spot.

The path leads alongside the church of St. Helen's, a pretty brick church built in the Gothic style in the last century, on the edge of the parkland of Biscathorpe House. The wooden bridge over the Bain here and the ford further along the lane can provide good venues for boat races or for the cooling of tired feet.

Route 6

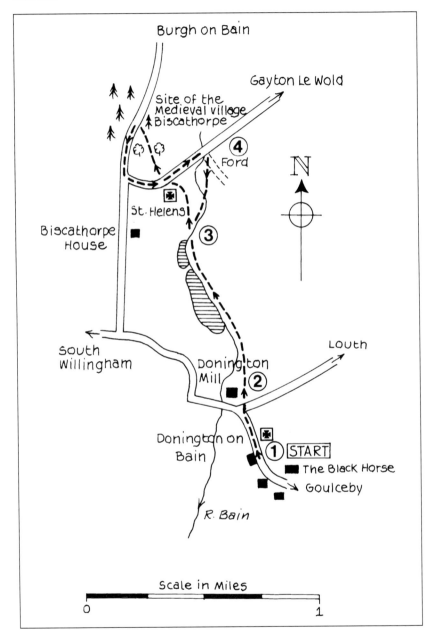

Burgh on Bain

Gayton Le Wold

Site of the
Medieval village
Biscathorpe

④ Ford

N

St. Helens

Biscathorpe
House

③

South
Willingham

Louth

Donington
Mill ②

Donington on
Bain

① START

The Black Horse

Goulceby

R. Bain

Scale in Miles

0   1

Route 6

Donington to Biscathorpe   3½ miles

Start

Donington on Bain lies approximately ten miles west of Louth off the A157. Park in the village, or in the car park of the Black Horse, with the kind permission of the landlord. GR 236828. Landranger series 122.

Route

1. *Turn right out of the car park and follow the village street past St. Andrew's Church. Turn right at the T-junction, then left along the Viking Way footpath.*

2. *Pass the water mill and follow the footpath along the riverbank. Pass the two fishing lakes. Just above the second lake follow the path right, then left over a stile.*

3. *Cross the footbridge over the Bain, go through the farm gate and walk towards St. Helen's Church. Bear right alongside the churchyard wall, go through the gate and across the lane. Cross the footbridge and walk straight up the field. Follow the footpath as it leads alongside the wood. Turn left at the lane and follow it back past St. Helen's Church and on over the ford.*

4. *Just beyond the ford, turn right onto a track, then bear right off the track towards the Bain. Step across to the opposite side and follow the bank to the bridge. Cross the bridge and retrace your steps along the footpath to Donington.*

Great Crested Grebe

31

Refreshments
There are plenty of picnic spots along the route, either on the river bank, beside the lakes or, perhaps best of all, at the ford at Biscathorpe. Alternatively, the Black Horse pub offers roaring fires and oak beams in cold weather or an attractive beer garden with children's play facilities in the summer. There is a good range of bar meals, family dining room and indoor recreational facilities – pool and pinball.

A path beside the River Bain.

Goulceby Village Walk

Outline
Three Horseshoes pub – Goulceby ford – The Viking Way – Goulceby Beck – The Reservoir – Sunnyside Farm – Goulceby ford – Three Horseshoes.

Summary
This is a good route for the very old and the very young. The footpaths lead through water meadows and along a stream bank, and wind between the cottages of Goulceby.

Attractions
A particular source of interest along the route is Goulceby Beck, which flows east to join the River Bain just beyond the village. The route leads alongside it at the ford, and then follows its course across the water meadows and back through the middle of the village. A fallen tree on the bank provides a good resting spot and opportunities for balancing acts.

Ladysmock and heartsease grow in the meadows in the early summer, while water forget-me-nots, bog-bean and mauve flowered water mints thrive in the gravelly bottom of the stream bed.

The small reservoir is home to Canada Geese, mallards, coots and moorhens, or water hens as they're known locally. Coots are identifiable by the white shield stretching from the bill to the top of the head – hence the expression 'as bald as a coot'. Nesting birds can be clearly observed here in the late spring, though of course care must be taken to avoid disturbing them.

Water Mint and Cucumber Dip
1 carton of set yoghurt
1 bunch of water mint, finely chopped
$1/2$ a cucumber, finely chopped

Mix the ingredients together and season to taste. Crushed garlic can be added. Use as a dip with sliced raw vegetables or pitta bread.

Route 7

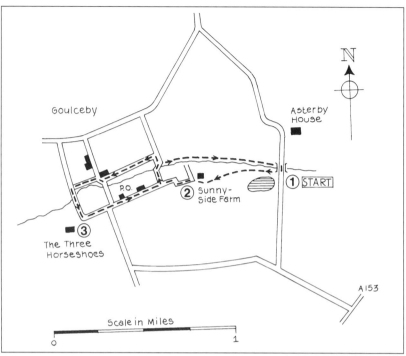

View across the Wolds.

Goulceby Village Walk   2 miles

Start

At Asterby. Six miles south of Louth on the A153 turn right for Goulceby. Take the first right hand turn and park in the lane just before the bridge. GR 253791. Landranger 122.

Route

1. *Face the bridge and turn left along the footpath. Follow the path up the bank alongside the wooden railing and then along the edge of the reservoir. Turn right alongside the next wooden railing, cross the stile and go over the footbridge. Walk on through the field keeping to the left of the hedge. At the end of the hedge bear slightly left then head straight on for Sunnyside Farm.*

2. *Pass Sunnyside Farm on your right and walk straight ahead down the lane. Take the first right hand turn. Cross the ford and then turn left. Follow the lane straight on ignoring the junction to left and right, until reaching a T-junction. Turn left for the Three Horseshoes.*

3. *Turn right out of the pub and follow the lane straight on past the Post Office. Turn left at the junction, go over the ford and look for a stile on the right way-marked the Viking Way. Cross the stile and follow the path diagonally right across the field. Cross the left hand stile, cross the track, go over the next stile and follow the path alongside the stream. On reaching the lane turn right and cross the bridge to finish.*

Refreshments

The Three Horseshoes is open at lunchtimes between Easter and October only. Sandwiches and bar meals are provided and can be eaten in the bar or outside at picnic tables in the adjoining camping field.

The village post office, alternatively, can provide picnic food which can be eaten on the banks of Goulceby Beck.

Hubbards Hills

Outline

Hubbards Hills car park – River Ludd – Hubbards Hills – Childrens play area and tea rooms – Riverside Park – Hubbards Hill Wood – Car park.

Summary

The route follows well-trodden paths through a recreational area bequeathed to the people of Louth early in the century. The River Ludd is shallow here and safe for paddling – there are plenty of minnows, so fishing nets may be a welcome addition to a picnic. These could be left in the car during the walk. There are river islands, small summerhouses and gazebos, waterfalls and stepping stones across the Ludd. Sheer chalk cliffs supporting massive beech trees form the sides of the valley here and create a stunning backdrop.

Attractions

The 35-acre stretch was bequeathed to the people of Louth in 1907 by a man named August Alphonse Pahud to the memory of his wife, Anne. There are fallen tree trunks to climb on and many little paths to explore, leading amongst the patches of woodland by the waterside.

To the north of the Ludd, Thorpe Hall can be seen – look out for deer in the grounds – a Fallow herd is bred commercially there. Thorpe Hall was built in the sixteenth century by Sir John Bolle, a young gallant who served under Elizabeth I at the seige of Cadiz in 1596. Whilst there a young Spanish lady fell in love with him but on learning that he had a wife in England she entered a nunnery and sent lavish gifts of jewels to the wife at Thorpe Hall, along with a painting of herself in a green dress. John Bolle's sons were Royalists during the Civil War and raised a regiment of foot soldiers at Thorpe Hall. The regiment fought for the king at Edgehill and finally met its end at Alton in Hampshire where it was decimated within the walls of the parish church. Colonel Bolle is said to have refused the offer of quarter and died in defence of his king, but not before putting six of his Roundhead adversaries to the sword.

The woodland path leads along the top of the high chalk cliff. Local boys can sometimes be seen riding their bikes down the almost sheer drop from the path to the valley bottom. Hair-raising to watch but apparently lots of fun!

Route 8

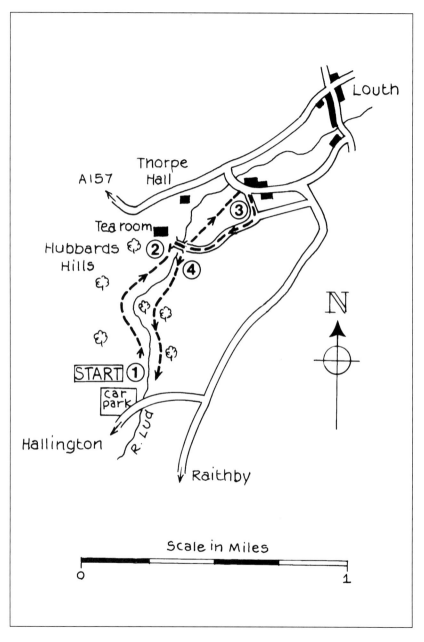

Route 8

Hubbards Hills   2 miles

Start

From Louth take the A157 West towards Welton-le-Wold. Hubbards Hills is sign posted to the left off this road and then to the right. The car park is about half a mile along the road from the second sign post. GR 315861. Landranger 122.

Route

1. *From the car park walk through into Hubbards Hills. Keep the River Ludd to your right and use one of the paths that follow the line of the river bank. Follow the river to the children's play area and tearooms, which are to the left of the main path.*

2. *Follow the path right over the bridge. Join the lane that bears left. Now follow the footpath that leads left into the park.*

3. *Walk across the park and turn right onto the lane. Turn right again at the junction. Follow the lane until just before the bridge.*

4. *Look out for a footpath leading left up into the woodland. Follow the path through the woods and on down the steps before arriving back at the car park.*

Refreshments

The Hubbards Hills Tearooms provide a variety of snacks and meals at reasonable prices. There is eating both inside and out, and an extensive childrens' play area.

There are plenty of picnic spots alongside the River Ludd.

Beech Noyau

Pack a jar with green beech leaves. Steep them in gin, cover with a lid and leave for a week. Strain the liquid. To each pint of liquid add 1 lb of sugar dissolved in $\frac{1}{2}$ pint of boiling water and 1 measure of brandy. Mix and bottle when cold.

Hubbards Hills.

Aby, Belleau and Claythorpe Mill

Outline

The Railway Tavern, Aby – The Great Eau – Manor Farm – St. John the Baptist's Church – Belleau – Claythorpe Watermill – Aby – The Railway Tavern.

Summary

This is a marsh walk involving two small villages, a church, streamside paths and a watermill.

Attractions

The Great Eau is a particularly lovely feature of the walk. It is fed in part by a spring that rises at Belleau and moves clean and swift over a gravelly bed between mints and water forget-me-nots. Swans nest here and can often be seen between the bridge and Manor Farm. Damsel flies fit amongst the reeds and overhanging willows. The Great Eau is fed by countless drains and dykes between here and Saltfleet and soon loses its early clean swiftness.

Belleau doesn't derive from 'beautiful water' as may be imagined, but from the Anglo Saxon 'Engelo', as it was registered in the Domesday Book, to 'Hellow' and then, perhaps in tribute to the water, to Belleau.

The Church of St. John the Baptist has some interesting features. The approach to the church is up a fairly steep bank, once a sea cliff, from which there is a fine view east across the marsh. The church is built of Spilsby greenstone and chalk. Inside there is the effigy of a knight, a crusader in armour and a surcoat, sword in hand, angels and a lion at his feet, that was found on the site of a Cistercian Priory at Aby. There is also a memorial to Sir Henry Vane, a seventeenth century owner of Belleau Manor who sailed to America and became Governor of Massachusetts. Harvard was founded during his time there, but on his return to England he was arrested and executed on a charge of High Treason.

The remains of Belleau Manor can be seen amongst the farm buildings. This was once a moated brick building, home of the Willoughby family. On one of the outside walls is the bust of a Wodewose, a wild man with bestial and erotic qualities, part of the Willoughby family emblem and intended to inspire fear and envy in rival families.

Claythorpe Mill is an eighteenth century watermill on the Great Eau. There are a variety of birds and animals to be seen in the grounds, and there is an 'enchanted woodland area', tea room and gift shop. There is an entry charge for children, but there is a good free view of the mill and the water fowl from the bridge.

The shorter return route is a pretty alternative, leading through wooded marshland.

Route 9

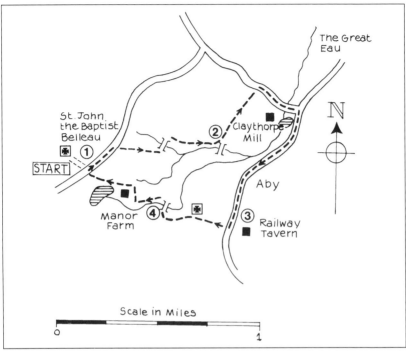

Swan on the Great Eau at Aby.

42

Route 9

Aby, Belleau and Claythorpe Mill   2 miles

Start

St. John the Baptist's Church, Belleau. Turn east off the A16, ten miles south of Louth, following the sign to South Thoresby and Aby. Continue to the fork in the road. Turn left here and then first right for Belleau. Park outside the church. GR 409784. Landranger 122.

Route

1. *With your back to the church turn left along the lane. Cross the bridge and look for a footpath sign pointing right. Head diagonally left across the field to the dyke. Cross at the footbridge and turn right. Follow the dyke to the next footbridge.*

2. *Do not cross the footbridge but look for a stile ahead. Cross this into the field, turn left into the adjoining field and follow the grass track to the lane. Turn right and continue past Claythorpe Mill. Follow the lane to a T-junction, then go right to Aby.*

3. *On the opposite side of the road to the Railway Tavern take the footpath that leads along the edge of the field. Go through the gate and into the churchyard. Keep to the left and go through the gap in the hedge to the next field. Turn left and go along the edge of the field. Turn right over a footbridge and left along the edge of the field.*

4. *Cross the bridge over the Great Eau, turn left and follow the path alongside the stream. Go through the gate and onto the track of Manor Farm. Follow the track past the old octagonal dovecote and onto the lane. St. John the Baptist's is above to the left. Return to start.*

Refreshments

The Railway Tavern provides a varied bar menu. There is a beer garden and children's play area. The tearoom at Claythorpe Mill provides drinks and snacks.

Claythorpe Mill.

44

South Thoresby to Swaby

Outline

The Vine, South Thorsby – Calceby Beck – Swaby Valley – Swaby Green Lane – Belleau Bridge – South Thoresby Church – The Vine.

Summary

This is an excellent walk for children of all ages. There is a good variety of landscape: meadow, stream bank, woodland, lakes, and plenty of climbing trees and bridges over Calceby and Swaby Beck.

Attractions

The Swaby Valley Nature Reserve is a steep-sided valley, uncharacteristic of the wolds and probably carved from the chalk by a glacial overflow. Chalk was quarried here until early in the century and used for building local houses. Look out for these in the village.

Calceby Beck flows through the valley and provides a habitat for king cups, yellow flags and butterbur, mints and water forget-me-not. According to Culpepper the root of the butterbur 'cures pestilential fevers and ... is very available against the plague, by provoking sweat'. The root, steeped in wine is also recommended as a cure 'for worms in the belly'.

Green winged orchids grow in the woodland bordering the Green Lane, and cowslips and self-heal thrive in the meadows.

Swaby is a pretty village with a duckpond set against a backdrop of white blackthorn in the late spring. A well placed bench provides a good picnic spot here. A conservation area has been developed along Church Lane in the village providing habitats for a variety of threatened bird and plant species.

Along the route look out particularly for long-tailed tits in the wooded areas, warblers in the valley itself and ptarmigan on the arable land that borders the Green Lane.

Route 10

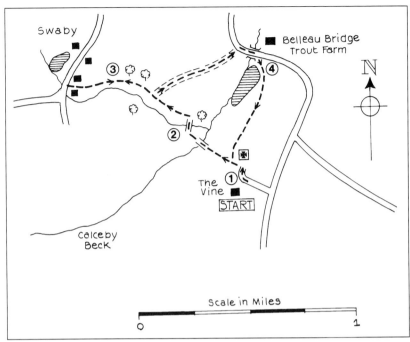

The duckpond.

46

Route 10

South Thoresby to Swaby   2 miles

Start

The Vine public house, South Thoresby. South Thoresby lies off the A16 about two and a half miles north of its junction with the A1104 beyond Alford. Park outside the pub. GR 402768. Landranger 122.

Route

1. *With your back to The Vine, turn left and then right at the end of the lane. Turn left just before the church and go through the farm gate. Go straight across the field and cross the stile. Cross the next stile, then cross the bridge over the stream. Continue across the field.*

2. *Bear right over the wooden bridge and follow the path round to the left. Pass the horse-chestnut trees on the right and keep straight on, ignoring the track on the right. Go through the wood and into Swaby Valley.*

3. *Follow the path along the valley bottom and out onto the lane. Continue along the lane to the duckpond. Retrace your steps through Swaby Valley to the Green Lane which leads off to the left of the path. Follow this track to the lane, then turn right.*

4. *Pass Belleau Bridge Trout Farm and turn right through the gate. Follow the path alongside the lakes before bearing left across the field to the church. Retrace your steps from here to The Vine.*

Refreshments

The Vine provides the usual range of bar meals and sandwiches. There is a particularly pretty beer garden, with childrens play equipment.

The butterbur

'The decoction of the root in wine is singularly good for those that wheeze much or are short winded. The powder of the root doth wonderfully help to dry up the moisture of sores that are hard to be cured and taketh away all spots and blemishes of the skin' – Culpepper.

Alford windmill.

Alford Town Walk

Outline

St. Wilfrid's Church – Alford windmill – Wold Grift Drain – Tothby Manor – Alford Manor House – St. Wilfrid's Church.

Summary

The route leads through the market town of Alford, with its five-sail working windmill, museum and craft market, and then out to some of the marsh meadows that surround the town. The footpath crosses Wold Grift Drain – one of the wider of the many ditches that have been used to reclaim the marsh land.

Attractions

Alford stands between the wolds and the sea, a marsh town that was settled before the Romans came. The town has had a market charter since the thirteenth century and has long been an important site for sheep and cattle fairs which used to be held in what is now Windmill Paddock. No doubt there were some riotous scenes to be witnessed there – markets were notorious for attracting rogues from all walks of life! These old fairs have now been replaced by an August Bank Holiday Arts Festival, a far more civilised affair, attracting some good quality musical and craft events and thousands of visitors.

Looking at Alford from Tothby Lane, the five-sail windmill dominates the town. In motion the sails seem part of a ritual, graceful and rhythmic, a living thing. Visitors are welcome in the windmill on Saturdays, occasional Sundays and on Bank Holidays. Up in the dome on a blustery day the building throbs to the rhythm of the sails, and the sacks of grain are hoisted up the centre of the building through a series of trap doors. Look down through the traps to the foreshortened visitors below! Outside on the platform the huge slatted sails pass so close to your face that you can feel the air move.

The mill grinds up to five tons of corn a day – flour and cakes can be bought here, and teas are served with delicious homemade flap jacks in the summer time.

The sixteenth century thatched manor house stands at the spot after which the town is named – the ford by the alder trees. The building is a folk museum displaying some interesting relics of the town's history and housing the Tourist Information Centre.

Smuggling was once rampant along the Lincolnshire coast and Alford was a popular spot for making deals and the exchange of contraband. Opposite St. Wilfrid's Church is Alford Coal Supplies, built on the site of the Old Red Lion. From the cellars here there are tunnels leading to 'The Hole in the Wall', between Market Place and the High Street. This was a drinking house of ill-repute, renowned as the haunt of smugglers. A skeleton with a knife is said to have been unearthed here during building restorations – plenty of room for speculation as to the grisly circumstances. Another skeleton was discovered in 1990, in the yard of Angeline's Pantry in the High Street – perhaps

(Continued on page 52)

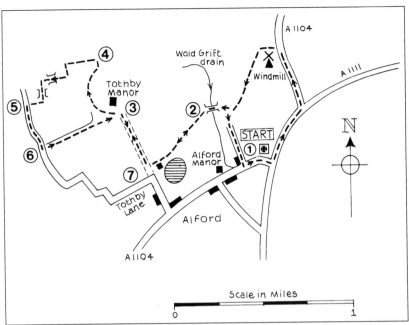

Stella, Rose, Bronwyn and Mum at the windmill.

Route 11

Alford Town Walk   4 miles

Start

At Alford, outside St. Wilfrid's Church. GR 455761. Landranger Series 122.

Route

1. *With your back to the church, turn left and walk away from the town. Keep to the left-hand pavement and follow the road to the windmill. Pass the windmill and turn left along the marked public footpath. Continue along the line of the hedge, bear slightly left and cross the stile. Go through the field and on to the gate. Cross the field and go through the gate. Head diagonally right across the field and go over the bridge.*

2. *Head straight across the field, then bear left to Gate Cottages. Just beyond the cottages follow the track right to Tothby Manor.*

3. *Cross the stile on the left, just before the gate into the Manor. Follow the path right, round the outskirts of the garden and through the orchard. Keep to the left of the wooden shed and continue to the stile. Cross the stile and the dyke and turn left along the edge of the field.*

4. *As the dyke leads left, cut right across the field following the yellow arrow. At the hedge turn left. Follow the hedge round the outskirts of the field until reaching a footbridge. Cross this and walk along the left-hand side of the field. Turn left over the bridge and then right for the lane.*

5. *Turn left at the lane.*

6. *After a quarter of a mile turn left along the footpath. Follow the path along the right hand side of the dyke. At the end of the field continue to follow the dyke towards Tothby Manor. Leave the dyke as it leads left. Follow the edge of the field to the track. Turn right at the track.*

7. *Turn left before the track joins Tothby Lane and follow the sign reading 'Public Footpath to Alford'. Follow this back to the bridge over Wold Grift Drain. Go right through the gate onto Park Lane. At the end of Park Lane turn left along the main street and arrive back at St. Wilfrid's Church.*

Refreshments

There is a wide choice of pubs and cafes in Alford. The Manor House provides a particularly scenic setting for light refreshment.

Route 11

(Continued from page 49)

another casualty of smuggling, or of the Bubonic Plague which swept Lincolnshire in the Middle Ages.

The wilder days of horse fairs and smuggling are long gone for Alford now. It's an attractive and peaceful market town, more or less unspoilt by modern shop frontages or by the tourist industry.

The lake at Well.

Well Vale

Outline

Skendleby Psalter – Fordington Wood – Badger Hill – St. Margaret's Church – Well Vale - Well – Forest Wood Ulceby – The Gate Inn – Skendleby Psalter.

Summary

Well Vale and its surrounding woods and uplands is claimed to be the most beautiful spot in the county. The horse chestnut trees in blossom in the early summer, lakes and parkland, a fine Grecian church on a hilltop, woods a mass of bluebells, the smell of wild garlic and the views across the marsh make the claim hard to refute.

Attractions

The bare spring earth of the Lincolnshire uplands provides a geological study of the wolds. The light brown earth, white in places is the soil of the chalk belt that curves from Dorset to East Anglia and then up to Yorkshire. Below the white chalk lies a layer of red chalk, its colour caused by the presence of iron, and below this a belt of carstone – russet coloured sandstone. The ploughed hillsides, then are rich spectrums of shades of brown.

In the late spring the woodland floors of Badger Hill are a myriad of bluebells. The azure haze reaches back amongst the trees, into the shadows of beech and ash, and in the foreground creates the texture of a seascape – blue beneath the white blossom of the blackthorn.

From Badger Hill on a clear day the North Sea can be seen far off across the marsh. To the south-east the north Norfolk cliffs rise on the far side of the Wash. In the near distance the stark outline of East Lindsay's nuclear fallout shelter contrasts with the softer lines of the wolds.

The path here leads alongside hedges of elder. The berries can sustain the thirsty in the autumn and the spring blossom can be gathered and used to make a refreshing, non-alcoholic elderflower champagne.

In St. Margaret's Churchyard there is the grave of a young gamekeeper William Dadley. The tale is told of how the young man on the evening of his wedding, heard the shots of poachers in the nearby woods. Leaving his guests and his young bride in the cottage he set off across the snow to tackle the men. Silhouetted against the white landscape, though, he was an easy target. He was shot dead as the poachers made their escape. Although his killer was never brought to justice, an Aby man confessed to the murder on his deathbed, many years later.

There are some wonderful climbing trees beside the lake, one of which has a particularly good swinging branch. There are an abundance of conkers to be gathered from the horse chestnut trees in the autumn.

Route 12

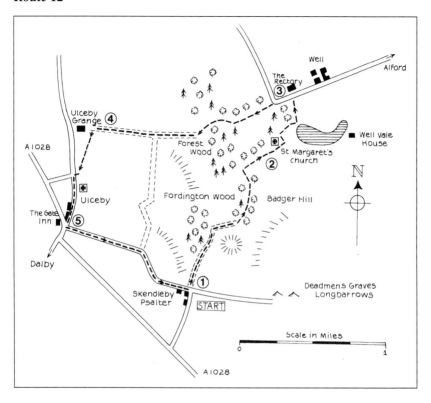

Route 12

Well Vale   4½ miles

Start

At Skendleby Psalter, a mile south-east of Ulceby and just north of the A1028. Park in the lay-by opposite the junction and next to the track. GR 435717. Landranger 122.

Route

1. Turn up the track opposite the junction. Follow the track along the edge of Fordington Wood, and turn right as it leads across the field. Bear left into the next piece of woodland. Follow the path through the wood and turn right at the junction of paths. Follow the path along the edge of the wood. Cross the stile and walk on to St. Margaret's Church.

2. Pass the church and go left down the hill towards the woodland. Turn right at the bottom of the hill and continue along the side of the lake. Turn left through the parkland. Turn left at the lane and continue to the sharp right-hand bend in the road.

3. Cross the stile straight ahead where the road bends sharp right. Follow the path through the wood for about half a mile. On leaving the wood take the track leading straight ahead across the farmland.

4. Before reaching the buildings of Ulceby Grange look for a stile on the left. Cross the stile and walk down the field, bearing slightly right. Cross the stile at the far side of the field, turn right onto the track, then left onto the lane. Pass the church and Glebe Farm. The Gate Inn is on the right on the far side of the road.

5. Turn left onto the lane immediately opposite the pub and return to Skendleby Psalter.

Refreshments

The Gate Inn provides particularly good value meals for children, along with more elaborate home cooked recipes. There is a large beer garden, complete with tethered goats and ponies in the spring and summer months.

Elderflower Fritters

1 cup of flour
1 egg
$1/2$ a cup of water
pinch of salt
elderflower heads

Make a batter from the flour, eggs, water and salt. Dip the elderflower heads into the batter, holding them by their stalks. Deep fry until golden brown. Drain them on kitchen paper and serve them hot, sprinkled with lemon and sugar.

Elderflower Champagne

5 heads of elderflowers in full bloom
1 gallon of cold water
1 lemon
$1 1/2$ lb of sugar
2 tablespoons of wine vinegar.

Put the elderflowers in a large jug along with the vinegar, the lemon juice and chopped up peel; dissolve the sugar in warm water, allow to cool and add to the other ingredients. Add the cold water. Cover with a loose cloth and leave for four days. Strain, and pour into screw top bottles. Drink chilled with slices of lemon.

Edwardian pillarbox.

Somersby, Tetford and the Roman Road

Outline

Hardens Gap – Warden Hill Farm – Somersby – The River Lymn – Tetford – The White Hart Inn – The Roman Road – Tetford Fen – Hardens Gap.

Summary

The route leads across the wooded flanks of Warden Hill and down into Somersby, the birthplace of Alfred Tennyson. 'Come from the woods that belt the grey hillside', asks the poet of his fading recollections of these childhood haunts in *Ode to Memory*. A bridge crosses the River Lymn just outside the village, and then the route continues to the village of Tetford, also on the Lymn, before leading back to Hardens Gap, following a stretch of Roman Road across Tetford Fen.

Attractions

The village of Somersby lies in the valley of the Lymn 'the brook that loves to purl over matted cress and ribbed sand or dimple in the dark of rushy coves'. Tennyson was born in the village and spent much of his childhood here, though his rural idyll was darkened by his father the rector who suffered severely from epilepsy and was an alcoholic: 'ever he muttered and maddened and ever wanned with despair'.

Tennyson went to Louth Grammar School at the age of seven. He hated the school and was unhappy in Louth. Because of the strain of his Somersby home he spent his holidays with an aunt in Mablethorpe and spent long summer days roaming the dunes of the Lincolnshire coast. He stayed intermittently at the Somersby rectory until 1837, his mother and the rest of the family having long since left to escape the rector. The rectory, now called Somersby House is up the lane behind the church but is not open to the public.

A winding leaf-dappled lane leads from the village and over the River Lymn. Just past the bridge at the Greetham turning, look left through the trees to Hoe Hill, an Iron Age long barrow thought to be of the Coritari people. They were finally conquered by the Romans around AD 50.

The stretch of Roman Road leading out of Tetford was part of a route leading from Lincoln to Skegness. Much of the route can still be traced – there is a six-mile stretch from Sotby to Belchford which is now a public bridleway. From Tetford the road perhaps crossed the ford at Brinkhill and continued on to Deersleap where it veered south-east towards Burgh le Marsh and Skegness. It seems that the road may have ended at a settlement, now lost, to the south of Skegness from where a ferry would have linked the trade route to Peddars Way in Norfolk. The Romans quarried their stone en route and so chalk pits are a regular feature on the road. One can be seen to the north of the road as it leads across Tetford Fen.

(Continued on page 60)

Route 13

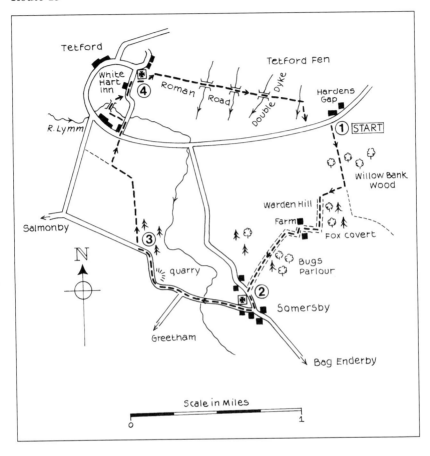

Tetford

Tetford Fen

White Hart Inn

④

Roman Road

Double Dyke

Hardens Gap

① START

R. Lymm

Willow Bank Wood

Warden Hill Farm

Fox Covert

Salmonby

③

Bugs Parlour

N

quarry

②

Somersby

Greetham

Bog Enderby

Scale in Miles

0   1

Route 13

Somersby, Tetford and the Roman Road   5 miles

Start

The walk starts mid-way between South Ormsby and Tetford. To get to South Ormsby turn south off the A16 about seven miles south of Louth. From South Ormsby on the Bluestone Heath Road take the road signposted to Brinkhill, then the first right turn. Continue for about one and a half miles until reaching footpaths leading left and right from the road. Park on the verge. GR 352743. Landranger 122.

Route

1 *Follow the footpath going south from the road. Take the first right-hand turn and walk through a field of crops. Now take a track leading left, alongside the woodland. Follow the track as it leads to the right and then on through Warden Hill Farm.*

2. *At the lane, turn left. Turn right through the churchyard and right at the lane. Continue for about half a mile along the lane. Immediately after a small pine wood turn right at a stile.*

3. *After crossing the stile, follow the footpath. Keep to the path as it forks right. At the lane turn left, then take the first lane on the right. Just before the bridge turn left into the field. Head for the far right-hand corner of the field. Go through the gate by the willow tree, cross the bridge and turn right. Walk through the field and out onto the lane. Turn left. Pass the White Hart Inn. At St. Mary's Church turn right into the churchyard.*

4. *Walk through the churchyard and cross the stile. Go straight on alongside the hawthorn hedge. Cross the stile and continue in a straight line over four footbridges, through two kissing gates and over one more bridge before turning right onto a track. Follow the track onto the lane then turn left and return to the car.*

Refreshments

The White Hart Inn provides a variety of bar meals and snacks. There is a beer garden with a good children's play area. Alternatively there is a suitable picnic spot in the meadow bordering the Lymn at Tetford.

Route 13

(Continued from page 57)

Leaving Tennyson and the Romans aside, there is plenty of more immediate interest along the route for young children. The path leads through patches of woodland – Willow Bank Wood, Fox Covert and the interestingly named Bug's Parlour! There are fossils to be found in the sandy quarry and there are a whole series of bridges, both over the Lymn and over the many dykes and drains of Tetford Fen. The second half of the route involves no uphill walking, so it should be manageable for fairly young children.

The Wolds in summer.

Bag Enderby to Stockwith Mill

Outline
St. Margaret's Church, Bag Enderby – River Lymn – Stainsby House – Nellspur – Green Lane – Stockwith Mill – Green Lane – River Lymn – Bag Enderby.

Summary
This is a route of varied landscape – streams, bridges, fords, Lincolnshire uplands and a stretch of Green Lane. The walk includes an old water mill by the side of Tennyson's 'brook', and there is a Viking shield boss in St. Margaret's Church.

Attractions
This route provides a full day out for an active family. There are streams along the way, with all the interest that water holds, from nature study to damming and paddling – the River Lymn cuts across the Green Lane and makes a particularly good spot for a rest and a picnic. There are fallen trees to climb on there and a bridge under which gruesome troll acts can be perfected.

Stockwith Mill is a seventeenth century water mill on the banks of the River Lymn. It was previously called Philip's Farm and seems to have been referred to by Tennyson in *The Brook*, which deals with the eternal nature of the river compared to man's mortality:

> I come from haunts of coot and hern
> I made a sudden sally
> And sparkle out among the fern
> To bicker down a valley.
>
> By thirty hills I hurry down
> Or slip between the ridges;
> By twenty thorps, a little town
> And half a hundred bridges.
>
> Till last by Philip's Farm I flow
> To join the brimming river
> For men may come and men may go
> But I go on for ever.

The 'brimming river' is presumably the River Steeping which has its confluence with the Lymn.

Whether the literary connection is genuine or not, the mill is worth a visit. Although

(Continued on page 64)

Route 14

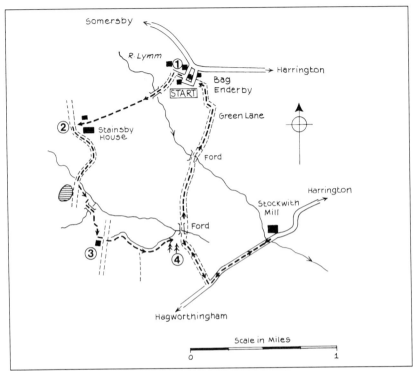

En route from Bagenderby to Stockwith Mill.

Route 14

Bag Enderby to Stockwith Mill   4¹/₂ miles

Start

From Hagworthingham on the A158 turn north. At the T-junction turn left to Bag Enderby. After half a mile turn left into the village and park outside the church. GR 349721. Landranger 122.

Route

1. *With your back to the churchyard gate turn right along the lane to a track on the left. Follow this to where another track joins on the left, then follow the latter to a right-hand bend in the track near a footbridge. Cross the footbridge, follow the path straight ahead, across the field then between the buildings of Stainsby House.*

2. *Turn left at the track and walk along it as far as the pond, then turn left keeping to the right of the stream. Cross the bridge and turn right. Follow the path left alongside the hedge, then turn left at the top of the field.*

3. *Turn right onto the track, pass Partridge Cottage, then turn immediately left. Follow the stream to the bottom of the field and then head right, through the coniferous trees and over the stile.*

4. *Turn right onto the Green Lane. Follow it to a junction with a lane Stockwith Mill is about half a mile down the lane on the left. Retrace your steps from the mill to the Green Lane. Follow this across the fords or footbridges and return to Bag Enderby.*

Refreshments

Stockwith Mill provides cooked meals and light refreshments, which can be eaten inside the mill or on wooden tables overlooking the mill pond.

Nettle Syrup

Boil 1 lb of young nettles to 2 pints of water, for one hour. Strain the liquid and add a pound of sugar to every pint of juice. Boil for a further ¹/₂ hour and then bottle in screw top jars.

The syrup is said to be an excellent tonic and blood purifier.

Route 14

(Continued from page 61)

it is no longer a productive mill, the old machinery is still in place and visitors are welcome to look at the workings. There is a craft shop and gift shop and, for those who are interested, a choice of short walks around the eighty acre site.

In St. Margaret's Church there is a Viking shield boss and a perpendicular octagonal font with some unusual representations of the pieta – Mary holding Jesus on her knee after the Crucifixion.

A scarecrow on the skyline.

Horncastle Canal Walk

Outline

Recreation ground – River Waring – Horncastle leisure centre and swimming pool – Horncastle canal – River Bain – leisure centre – River Waring – Recreation ground.

Summary

The canal at Horncastle was built in the nineteenth century for the transportation of grain to the east coast. Now that it is no longer used for trading purposes there are plans afoot to develop it as a tourist canal. In the meantime it provides habitats for grebes, coots and moorhens and occasional flocks of Canada geese. Reed buntings and reed warblers nest in the reed beds alongside the canal.

Attractions

Horncastle lies between the two wolds rivers, the Bain and the Waring, both of which were diverted during the building of the canal. The route begins by following the Waring along its original course, upstream from the swings and slides. Its banks here are now a public park – as well as the children's playground there is a swimming pool and leisure centre.

Having crossed the bridge over the canal, the route leads alongside the old railway line. The old station yard is now a builders merchants in the centre of town. Most of Lincolnshire's railways were closed in the sixties and seventies during a controversial cost-cutting exercise by British Rail. Reed beds have formed below the old line – bull-rushes grow here and clumps of yellow flag in the early summer.

Halfway up the footpath is the old lock – the original stonework is still in place. Notice the evenly placed holes in the stonework – the bargepoles would have been pushed into these to propel the barge along through the lock, the water levels being too low for the horse to have remained safely harnessed.

On the east bank the original line of the River Bain can be seen. This is dry now and overhung by some good climbing trees. Beyond, crops of flax are grown for the linseed oil. The flowers bloom in the late spring and create a spectacular blue haze stretching away to the outskirts of the town. Crush the seeds between your fingers in the autumn and smell the oil.

The name Horncastle is thought to derive from Hyrn-ceaster, the 'camp on the horn', because of the town's position on a 'horn' between the two rivers. The Romans were thought to have called the town Banovallum. Although the name is now disputed by local historians, there is no doubt that there was a Roman settlement here. The remains of the Roman wall can still be seen at the end of Manor House Street, beyond the church of St. Mary. The wall now forms part of the footings for the local community centre!

(Continued on page 68)

Route 15

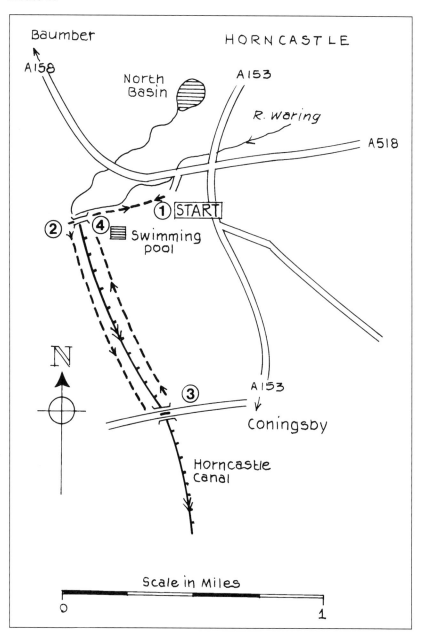

Baumber
HORNCASTLE
A158
North
Basin
A153
R. Waring
A518
① START
② ④ Swimming
pool
N
③ A153
Coningsby
Horncastle
Canal
Scale in Miles
0
1

Route 15

Horncastle Canal Walk   2 miles

Start

Coming from Coningsby on the A153, enter the town and turn left towards Baumber. Turn left again into a road named Cagthorpe. Park beside the swings. GR 257694. Landranger 122.

Route

1. *Turn left out of the recreation ground and follow the riverside path. Pass the leisure centre and swimming pool on your left, cross the footbridge, and turn left alongside the canal.*

2. *Follow the towpath that leads between the canal and the disused railway-line. Pass the old lock. At the lane turn left, cross the bridge, then turn left along the east bank of the canal.*

3. *Walk on down the towpath, pass the course of the River Bain on your right and return to the swimming pool.*

4. *Retrace your steps along the bank of the River Waring and back to the start.*

Refreshments

There are plenty of cafes and restaurants in Horncastle. There is a particularly nice fish and chip cafe, the Mermaid Fishery, next to the Town Hall.

Cinder Tea

Make a cup of black tea and stand it on the hearth. Heat a poker in the hot coals of the fire. When red hot, plunge it into the tea. This is said to be an excellent remedy for a chesty cough.

Route 15

(Continued from page 65)

Horncastle is one of the few Roman settlements in Lincolnshire to have had a defensive wall. This was built at the end of the Roman period, just before the legions returned to Rome. The Friesans, Saxons and Angles who came in their place settled and farmed the countryside and the towns were left to decay.

Two pretty blue and white cottages stand behind St. Mary's Church. Unexpectedly, one of these was the old workhouse and the other was a dispensary of medicine for the poor in the eighteenth century, the first of its kind in Lincolnshire.

In the centre of the town, adjoined to a proud Georgian terrace is an unspeakably ugly Woolworths. This was built on the site of Sellwood House, the girlhood home of Emily Sellwood, wife of Alfred Tennyson. There are plenty of other fine examples of Georgian architecture throughout the town, and very many antique and second-hand shops in which to brouse.

The north basin of the Horncastle canal is now a pleasant grassy area, home to various exotic ducks. The old water mill is still standing, though no longer functional – look for the mark of the old mill wheel above the water line.

Reedwarbler.

Bratoft and Gunby Hall

Outline

Whitegates Cottage – Dismantled railway – Gunby Park – The Sun Inn – Whitegates Cottage.

Summary

This is a marsh walk across National Trust Land. The route includes an old mud and stud cottage which is open to the public, a stretch of disused railway line, a railway museum and the parkland of Gunby Hall, roughly one mile S.E. of Bratoft Ings, a Scandinavian word for low lying meadows, which now belongs to the Lincolnshire Trust.

Attractions

There are glimpses of Gunby Hall, home of the Massingberd family, along the course of the route, from the railway line and from the scattered copses of the parkland. The hall was built in the seventeenth century for the family, who previously lived in Bratoft. It is now the property of the National Trust and is open to the public on Wednesday afternoons between March and September.

There is a curse on the Massingberd family. In the eighteenth century a daughter fell in love with one of the Gunby stable hands and planned to elope with him. Her father learnt of the attachment and shot the young man. His daughter put a curse on the family, that there would never be a direct line of inheritance through the male line – and the curse must have been a powerful one, as this has held true to the present day.

Bratoft Ings (see the map) is a small nature reserve, also known as Heath's Meadows, after a Nurse Heath of Nettleton who helped to raise the money for the site. The Ings are mown according to traditional methods, and the grassland provides habitats for many threatened species of meadow flower, including the green winged orchid.

Whitegates Cottage is a traditional mud and stud cottage, a style which was once common in Lincolnshire but which is now rare. The cottage has a long straw thatched roof. It was recently restored using traditional methods and materials. It is open to the public, but only by appointment with the tenant, Mr. Zaremba, of Whitegates Cottage, Mill Lane, Gunby Hall Estate, Bratoft, Nr. Spilsby.

Route 16

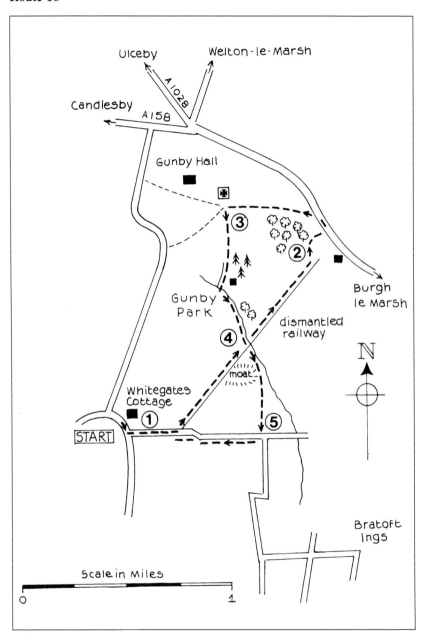

Route 16

Bratoft and Gunby Hall   4 miles

Start

From Candlesby on the A158 Horncastle to Skegness road go east for about half a mile. Before reaching the roundabout turn right along an unclassified road. Continue to a junction and turn left. Whitegates Cottage is along the lane on the left. Park outside the cottage. GR 463652. Landranger 122.

Route

1. *Continue past Whitegates Cottage and turn left. Turn left onto the disused railway line and follow this for one mile. At the end of the line turn left over the stile, then go diagonally right up the field. Go over the stile and into the wood.*

2. *Go through the wood, then straight across the field to the next stile. Turn left at the road and continue to a stile on your left. Cross this and follow the path as it leads along the edge of the wood. Go straight on across the parkland to the church.*

3. *From the church turn left, down the open parkland. Aim to the right of the small patch of coniferous woodland. Cross the stile and pass a cottage on the left. Continue to the next stile. Cross this, bear slightly left and then turn left following a drainage ditch. At the patch of woodland bear right for the dismantled railway line.*

4. *Cross the railway line by the stile and continue along the line of the hedge to the next stile. Pass the remains of the moat and continue to the lane. Turn right and continue to Whitegates Cottage.*

Buttercup ointment

Heat a cupful of vaseline in a saucepan along with as many freshly picked buttercup heads as can be blended in. After 15 minutes strain the hot ointment through muslin into small screw top jars. Use when cold for all skin complaints.

Old Bolingbroke Village Walk

Outline
Hagnaby Lane – The Brook – Old Water Mill – Bolingbroke Castle – St. Mary's Church – The Black Horse Inn – Grove Farm – Hagnaby Lane.

Summary
This easily managed route leads through the village streets of Old Bolingbroke, past the ruins of the famous castle, alongside the brook and the old mill, and includes a particularly good pub, The Black Horse Inn.

Attractions
Old Bolingbroke Castle was the home of John of Gaunt and the birthplace of Henry IV. Geoffrey Chaucer was a frequent visitor here. He was a favourite of John of Gaunt and wrote an early poem, 'The Deth of Blanche the Duchesse' on the death of his patron's first wife, the mother of Henry.

John of Gaunt extended the castle and built the greenstone church. The path between the castle and the church must often have been walked by these old Lancastrians during the troubled reign of Richard II – the family emblem, the Lancaster Rose can be seen outside the Black Horse Inn.

The castle was a Royalist stronghold during the Civil War but surrendered to the Cromwellians after the battle of Winceby in 1643. It then fell rapidly into a state of ruin – the final walls collapsed completely in 1815. The ruins have now been carefully excavated and make interesting study, particularly on a sunny day when the grassy banks make inviting spots to sit and rest.

A brook winds its way through the village, in and out of the pond and past an old water mill. Old Bolingbroke is now a conservation area, with some particularly pretty cottages, surrounded by narrow winding lanes and the gently rolling hillsides.

Refreshments
The Black Horse Inn provides bar snacks and welcome children. There is a pleasant seating area outside.

Route 17

Old Bolingbroke Village Walk   1 mile

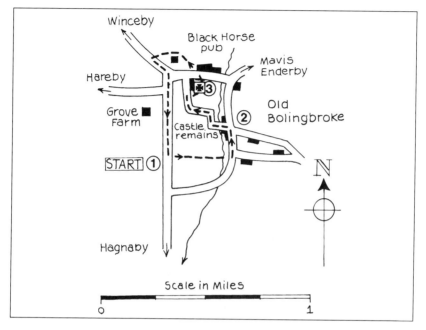

Start

Old Bolingbroke lies three miles west of Spilsby off the A1115. Park the car on the lane to Hagnaby just beyond Grove Farm. GR 348648. Landranger 122.

Route

1. Look for a public footpath sign pointing left off the lane just beyond the castle grounds. Cross the field and go over the footbridge. Turn left at the lane.

2. Take the first lefthand turn and follow the lane past the mill and to the entrance to the castle. From here continue along the lane. Turn right along a track leading to the churchyard. Go through the churchyard and out onto the lane.

3. Cross the lane and take a track leading straight ahead alongside Dewy House.

4. Keep to the track as it leads round to the left past the bungalow and on down to the lane. Turn left and walk back to the village. The Black Horse pub is just beyond the war memorial. Take the right hand turn at the war memorial, for Hagnaby. Walk on and arrive back at the car.

73

Little Cawthorpe Village Walk

Outline
The Royal Oak – Village duckpond – Wood Lane – The Splash – St. Helen's Church –
The Royal Oak.

Summary
This is a nice, easy walk for young children. The route leads past a duckpond across
small meadows and alongside the longest splash in the country, before following the
stream between cottage gardens and returning to the pub.

Attractions
A local man, John Davies, lives in a bungalow with a beautiful garden beside the
splash. He has this tale to tell:

'A few years ago two men came to my house and asked if this was a main road
outside. I told them that it was and one of the men told me that he was from the BBC
and that there would be a film crew there in the morning. Sure enough at 9 o'clock in
the morning, there they were, filming. This chap reversed his car into the splash; and
they filmed him driving out, in his open topped MGB. Then he got my son to show him
the way in from the other end and they filmed him driving in for about 12 ft. And when
it came out on the television it looked as though he'd driven right the way through in an
open topped sports car. So the following weekend we had seventeen vehicles stuck in
the splash here. I can still hear them all saying 'But that chap from the BBC did it!' '

Which just goes to show that you can't believe everything you see on the telly!

Look out for minnows as you walk alongside the splash. You may be lucky enough
to see a tawny owl roosting amongst the trees on the far side. The village pond is a
popular nesting spot for waterfowl – there is a conveniently placed bench from which
to watch them.

The church of St. Helens is worth a visit to see the particularly interesting
Romanesque frieze.

Refreshments
The Royal Oak has a large beer garden with children's play equipment. There is a
special children's bar menu, along with a range of adult meals and snacks.

Route 18

Little Cawthorpe Village Walk   1¹/₂ miles

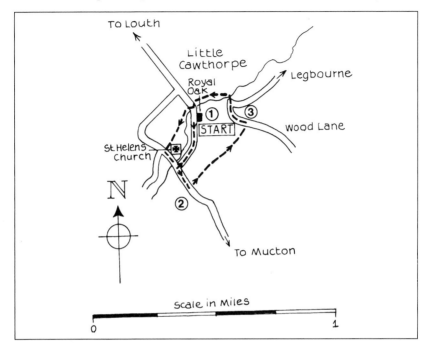

Start

Little Cawthorpe lies just beyond Legbourne off the A157 Louth to Mablethorpe road. Park at the Royal Oak pub, in the centre of the village. GR 358841. Landranger 113.

Route

1. *Walk out of the pub car park and turn left onto the lane. Follow the lane past the cottages and duckpond and turn left at the junction.*

2. *Walk on until reaching a gate into the field on the left. Bear slightly left across the field to a bridge. Walk ahead alongside the hedge to another bridge. Cross this and cross the stile. Bear right, cross the stile and follow the hedgerow to the lane.*

3. *Turn left down Wood Lane, then left again alongside the splash. At the end of the splash turn left towards the pub, then immediately right along a narrow footpath. Follow this alongside the stream, past the gardens and through the meadow. Turn left onto the lane. Turn left again past the church and return to The Royal Oak.*

Look out for Victorian pillarboxes, they are common in the Wolds.

Useful information

Animals and Wildlife
Animal Gardens, Mablethorpe. 01507 473346. This is an animal sanctuary providing treatment for injured animals and birds.

Claythorpe Mill and Wildlife Gardens, 01507 450687. The mill is near the village of Aby, Alford, and stands on the banks of the Great Eau. There is a good variety of wild fowl to be seen here, along with friendly farm animals. There is a tea room and a gift shop and a woodland play area. The mill is open from March to October from 10–6. Admission: adults £2.55, children £1.75.

Elsham Hall Country and Wildlife Park, Elsham, Brigg. 01652 688698. The Park is set in the lakeside grounds of Elsham Hall and includes a falconry centre, garden centre, carp pond, adventure playground and a small farm. Full meals and light refreshments are available. The Park is open daily from Easter to mid-September and on Sundays only from mid-September to Easter. Admission: adults £4, children £2.50.

Fenside Goat Centre, Chestnut Lodge, Fenside, Toynton-All-Saints, Spilsby. 01790 52452. A variety of goats here to look at and feed, and a selection of goats milk products on sale. Opening times are variable throughout the year so it is a good idea to telephone in advance. Admission: adults £1.80, children £1.00.

Hedgehog Care, the Post Office, Authorpe, Louth. 01507 450221. An extraordinary example of self sacrifice and devotion to the care of hedgehogs. The owners have given over their home to tend any injured hedgehog, and casualties are admitted at any time of the day or night. There is also a hedgehogs Garden of Rest. Admission is free, but any donations to the cause are acceptable.

Horse World, Sand Lane, Osgodby, Market Rasen. 01673 843407. Horse rides and pony-cart rides along with pre-booked riding lessons available. There are working horses to be seen and a bird of prey sanctuary to visit. Horse World is open throughout the year, from 10 am – 8 pm. Admission: adults £2, children £1.

Northcote Heavy Horse Centre, Great Steeping, Spilsby. 01754 830286. A working horse centre. Visitors are expected to get involved with the everyday tasks. There is a cafe and a picnic area and a gift shop. The centre is open throughout the year, but it is advisable to check specific details beforehand. Admission: adults £4, children £2.80.

Natureland Seal Sanctuary, North Parade, Skegness. 01754 764345. Cares for injured seals and helps them to re-adjust to life in the wild. The centre also houses alligators, snakes, turkeys and goats and has an amazing butterfly house. There is a children's play area and a tearoom. The sanctuary is open all year round, but the butterflies can only be seen from May to September. Admission: adults £3.20, children £2.10.

Bicycle Hire
Jubilee Park, Woodhall Spa. 01526 352448

Cinemas and theatres
The Phoenix Cinema, Raynard Street, Spilsby. 01790 753675
The Regal Cinema, West Street, Boston. 01205 350553
The Tower Cinema, Skegness. 01754 763938
The Kinema in the Woods, Woodhall Spa. 01526 352166
Elsham Hall Barn Theatre, Elsham, Brigg. 01652 688698
Spilsby Theatre, Church Street, Spilsby. 01790 752936
The Playgoers Theatre, Newmarket, Louth. 01507 603549

Crafts
Alford Craft Market and Shop, Newmarket, Louth.
Alford Pottery, The Pottery, Commercial Road, Alford.
Alvingham Pottery and Crafts, Yarborough Road, Alvingham, Louth. 01507 327230.
Brinkhill Pottery, Brinkhill near Alford.

Mayfield Court Crafts, 104, High Street, Broughton, Brigg. 01652 658172.

Historic Buildings
Bolingbroke Castle, Old Bolingbroke, Spilsby.
Gunby Hall, Spilsby. Open from April to September, Wednesday and Thursday afternoons.
Tattershall Castle, Tattershall, Lincoln. 01526 342543.

Leisure Centres
Bainland Country Park, Woodhall Spa. 01526 352903. A countryside holiday centre with an 18-hole golf course, tennis courts, bowling green and croquet lawn. There is an indoor heated swimming pool, a solarium, jacuzzi and a sauna. Family day memberships are available throughout the year.
Woodthorpe Hall Leisure Park, Woodthorpe, Alford. 01507 450294. Woodthorpe Hall offers an 18-hole golf course and all-weather bowling green. There is also a lake, with wheelchair access, an aquatic centre, garden centre and childrens play area. The Woodthorpe Country Inn offers a restaurant and family room.

Mills
Alford Windmill, 32, East Street, Alford. 01205 352188. This is still a working mill. There are regular open days throughout the year, on which freshly milled flour can be bought. Cream teas and locally made cakes are served.
Alvingham Watermill, Church Lane, Alvingham, Louth. 01507 327544. The mill has regular open days throughout the summer months. There is a picnic area but no refreshments are available.
Claythorpe Mill, (see Animals and Wildlife).
Stockwith Mill, Harrington Road, Hagworthingham, Spilsby. 01507 588221. A water mill on the banks of the River Steeping. It is no longer a working mill but the old mill machinery is intact and can be seen on open days. The mill is open to the public from Easter to October, Tuesday to Sunday and on Bank Holiday Mondays.
Wrawby Postmill, Mill Lane, Wrawby, Brigg. 01652 653699. This was the last working post mill in the North of England. It has a number of open days throughout the summer.
Burgh-le-Marsh Windmill, Burgh-le-Marsh. A working windmill with five sails.

Museums
Baysgarth House Museum, Caistor Road, Barton on Humber. 01652 632318. The museum is open on Thursdays, Fridays and Bank Holidays from 10 am – 4 pm and on Saturdays and Sundays from 10 am – 5 pm. It is closed over the Christmas period.
Legbourne Railway Museum, The Old Station, Legbourne, Louth. 01507 603116. The museum is inside the restored railway building of Louth Station. There is a signal box and a vast amount of railway memorabilia. Children can operate a model railway, and there is a play area and a pets corner. The museum opens from Easter to 30th September, 10.30 am – 5 pm.
Louth Museum, 4 Broadbank Louth. 01507 601211. The museum is open from 1st March to 29th November, on Wednesdays, Fridays, Saturdays and Sundays, from 2 pm – 4 pm.
The Manor House, West Street, Alford. 01507 466488. The Manor House is open from Monday to Saturday, 10 am – 5 pm, and on Sunday from 1.30 – 4.30 pm.
Woodhall Spa Cottage Museum, Iddesleigh Road, Woodhall Spa. 01526 353775. The museum is open from Easter to October, Monday to Saturday, from 10–5, and on Sunday from 11–5.
Church Farm Museum, Church Road, Skegness. 01754 766658. A preserved farmhouse, cottage and farm buildings. There are various displays throughout the year.

Nature Reserves
Snipe Dales, Near Hagworthingham on the A158. Wooded banks rise steeply from the valley bottom. Snipe and woodcock nest here amongst the bracken.
The Battle of Winceby was fought near here in Slash Hollow in 1643 as Parliament troups

headed for Old Bolingbroke Castle.

Gibraltar Point, Three miles south of Skegness, winding paths lead out between sand dunes onto salt marsh. In the spring and summer the air is vibrant with sky lark's song and the ground a purple carpet of sea lavender. Later in the year sea birds and waders flock here in their thousands, either on passage to warmer climates or to spend the winter.

From the highest dunes on a clear day you can see south to the Norfolk cliffs, on the far side of the Wash, and north-west to the wolds rising from the marsh.

Red Hill, Three miles south-east of Donington on Bain. The reserve has been developed around a disused chalk quarry. The workings reveal clearly the layers of rock that make up the wolds, rust coloured sandstone is topped by red chalk, over the top of which is a layer of white chalk.

The reserve is a mass of grassy hollows on the steep side of Red Hill – hawthorn and blackthorn line the top of the quarry. Because of the steep sided nature of the hill it has never been farmed and consequently its flora has been undisturbed for centuries. Orchids, gentian and rock rose grow in profusion here. There are spectacular views to the south-west, across the wolds.

Donna Nook, Near North Somercotes on the A1051. The main attraction at Donna Nook is the colony of seals that lives and breeds here, seemingly unaffected by the noise of the nearby firing range!

Play Centres

Kids Kingdom, Manby Park, Manby, Louth. 01507 327358. An adventure play centre on two floors, with indoor and outdoor facilities. There are inflatables, climbing equipment, swings and slides, a baby area and refreshments. The centre closes for one week over Christmas.

Panda's Palace, Tower Esplanade, Skegness. 01754 765494. A wonderful children's activity centre, with inflatables and ball pools.

Public Transport
Bus Companies
Louth, Road Car. 01507 600364
Lincoln, Road Car. 01522 832424
Skegness, Road Car. 01754 763365
Boston, Briar Lane Travel. 01205 364087
Mablethorpe, Gracecroft Coaches. 01507 473236
Alford, Hunts. 01507 463478
Market Rasen, Blanchards. 01673 842205

Swimming Pools
Funcoast World, Skegness. 01754 765567. An Hawaiian beach theme pool, with slides, fountains, whirlpools etc.
Louth Swimming Pool, 01507 604738
Horncastle Swimming Pool, 01507 522489
Jubilee Park Woodhall Spa, 01526 352448. There is an outdoor pool here which is open during the summer months.

Tourist Information Offices
Louth Tourist Information, 01507 609289
Skegness Tourist Information, 01754 764821
Alford Tourist Information, 01507 462143
Market Rasen Tourist Information, 01673 842479

THE FAMILY WALKS SERIES

Family Walks on Anglesey. Laurence Main	ISBN 0 907758 66 5
Family Walks around Bakewell & Castleton. Norman Taylor	ISBN 0 907758 37 1
Family Walks in Berkshire & North Hampshire. Kathy Sharp	ISBN 0 907758 37 1
Family Walks around Bristol, Bath & the Mendips. Nigel Vile	ISBN 0 907558 19 3
Family Walks around Cardiff & the Valleys. Gordon Hindess	ISBN 0 907758 54 1
Family Walks in the Cotswolds. Gordon Ottewell	ISBN 0 907758 15 0
Family Walks in the Dark Peak. Norman Taylor	ISBN 0 907758 16 9
Family Walks in Dorset. Nigel Vile	ISBN 0 907758 86 X
Family Walks in East Sussex. Sally & Clive Cutter	ISBN 0 907758 71 1
Family Walks on Exmoor & the Quantococks. John Caswell	ISBN 0 907758 46 0
Family Walks in Gower. Amanda Green	ISBN 0 907758 63 0
Family Walks in Gwent. Gordon Hindess	ISBN 0 907758 87 8
Family Walks in Hereford and Worcester. Gordon Ottewell	ISBN 0 907758 20 7
Family Walks on the Isle of Man. John Kitto	ISBN 0 907758 91 6
Family Walks on the Isle of Wight. Laurence Main	ISBN 0 907758 56 8
Family Walks around Keswick and Northern Lakeland. Timothy and Sylvia Bunker	ISBN 0 907758 93 2
Family Walks in the Lake District. Barry McKay	ISBN 0 907758 40 1
Family Walks in Leicestershire. Meg Williams	ISBN 0 907758 82 7
Family Walks in Lincolnshire. Camilla Harrison	ISBN 0 907758 67 3
Family Walks in Mendip, Avalon & Sedgemoor. Nigel Vile	ISBN 0 907758 41 X
Family Walks in Mid Wales. Laurence Main	ISBN 0 907758 27 4
Family Walks in the New Forest. Nigel Vile	ISBN 0 907758 60 6
Family Walks on the Norfolk Broads. Norman Taylor	ISBN 0 907758 90 8
Family Walks in Northamptonshire. Gordon Ottewell	ISBN 0 907758 81 9
Family Walks in the North Wales Borderlands. Gordon Emery	ISBN 0 907758 50 9
Family Walks on the North Wales Coast. Gordon Emery	ISBN 0 907758 89 4
Family Walks in North West Kent. Clive Cutter	ISBN 0 907758 36 3
Family Walks in North Yorkshire Dales. Howard Beck	ISBN 0 907758 52 5
Family Walks in Oxfordshire. Laurence Main	ISBN 0 907758 38 X
Family Walks in Pembrokeshire. Laurence Main	ISBN 0 907758 75 4
Family Walks in Snowdonia. Laurence Main	ISBN 0 907758 32 0
Family Walks in South Derbyshire. Gordon Ottewell	ISBN 0 907758 61 4
Family Walks in South Shropshire. Marian Newton	ISBN 0 907758 30 4
Family Walks in South Yorkshire. Norman Taylor	ISBN 0 907758 25 8
Family Walks in the Staffordshire Peaks & Potteries. Les Lumsdon	ISBN 0 907758 34 7
Family Walks around Stratford & Banbury. Gordon Ottewell	ISBN 0 907758 49 5
Family Walks in Suffolk. C. J. Francis	ISBN 0 907758 64 9
Family Walks in Surrey. Norman Bonney	ISBN 0 907758 74 6
Family Walks around Swansea. Raymond Humphreys	ISBN 0 907758 62 2
Family Walks in the Teme Valley. Camilla Harrison	ISBN 0 907758 45 2
Family Walks in Three Peaks & Malham. Howard Beck	ISBN 0 907758 42 8
Family Walks in the Weald of Kent & Sussex. Clive Cutter	ISBN 0 907758 51 7
Family Walks in West London. Caroline Bacon	ISBN 0 907758 72 X
Family Walks in West Sussex. Nick Channer	ISBN 0 907758 73 8
Family Walks in West Yorkshire. Howard Beck	ISBN 0 907758 43 6
Family Walks in the White Peak. Norman Taylor	ISBN 0 907758 90 6
More Family Walks in the White Peak. Norman Taylor	ISBN 0 907758 80 0
Family Walks in Wiltshire. Nigel Vile	ISBN 0 907758 21 5
Family Walks in the Wye Valley. Heather & Jon Hurley	ISBN 0 907758 26 6
Family Walks in Birmingham & West Midlands.	ISBN 0 907758 83 5

If you have written a definitive book of regional interest, we may be interested in publishing it – please write or send a synopsis.

Scarthin Books of Cromford, in the Peak District, are also leading new, second-hand and antiquarian booksellers, and are eager to purchase specified material, both ancient and modern.

Contact Dr. D. J. Mitchell 01629 823272.